Your WRITE Calling

Is Writing Right for You?

"This small volume packs a lot of practical advice in a handy format. Ingest it and watch your writing improve."
**Jerry B. Jenkins, Novelist & Biographer
Owner, Christian Writers Guild**

Your Write Calling:
Is Writing Right for You?
by Beyr Reyes, PhD
Copyright @ 2012 ShadeTree Publishing, LLC
Print ISBN: 978-1-937331-41-2
e-Book ISBN: 978-1-937331-42-9

Scripture quotations marked "NIV" are taken from the HOLY BIBLE, NEW INTERNATIONAL VERSION®. Copyright © 1973, 1978, 1984 International Bible Society. Used by permission of Zondervan. All rights reserved.

Scripture quotations marked "NKJV" are taken from the New King James Version®. Copyright © 1982 by Thomas Nelson, Inc. Used by permission. All rights reserved.

Scripture quotations marked "KJV" are taken from the King James Version. The KJV is public domain in the United States.

Scripture quotations marked "NET" are taken from the NET Bible® copyright ©1996-2006 by Biblical Studies Press, L.L.C. http://netbible.com All rights reserved.

All rights reserved. This book is protected by copyright. No part of this book may be reproduced or transmitted in any form or by any means, electronic or mechanical, including photocopying, recording, or by any information storage and retrieval system, without permission in writing from the publisher.

The purpose of this book is to educate and enlighten. This book is sold with the understanding that the publisher and author are not engaged in rendering counseling, albeit it professional or lay, to the reader or anyone else. The publisher and author shall have neither liability nor responsibility to any person or entity with respect to any loss or damage caused, or alleged to have been caused, directly or indirectly, by the information contain in this book.

Visit our Web site at
www.ShadeTreePublishing.com

Introduction	1
Are You Called?	3
How People Receive Their Calling	7
God Will Equip You	13
How to Know What to Write	21
What It Means to Be a Writer for God	29
Choose Your Path Wisely	37
Questions and Reflections	43
About the Author	53
References	58

INTRODUCTION

*Everyone has a book inside of them,
but not everyone is called by God
to be a writer for Him.*

– Beyr Reyes

If I've talked to 1000 people about being a writer, then 998 of them have told me that they are supposed to write a book about their life. Does this number seem strangely large to you? Well, it doesn't to me.

Jesus commanded His children to preach to people and to testify about Him.[1] We as Christians are called to convey the gospel of God's love, mercy, and grace, especially in our own lives. Therefore, it should not be a surprise that most Christians in the world feel some sort of inclination to share their story. If they don't, then maybe their heart is not where it should be.

Being called to share your testimony (by mouth, by pen, or by keyboard) is not the same thing as being called by God to be a writer for Him. There *is* a difference. If you don't know which category befits you, then this book will help you to decide. On the other hand, if you know without a doubt that you are called to write for God, then this book

Beyr Reyes, PhD

will open your eyes to what that entails and what awaits you.

Your WRITE Calling

ARE YOU CALLED?

The Lord has plans for us. It's just that simple. The Lord says that before He formed us in our mother's womb, He knew us, and before we were born, He set us apart and appointed us.[2] His plans are to prosper us, not to harm us, but give us hope and a future.[3]

As the Psalmists so eloquently put it:

> *Many, O Lord my God, are the wonders you have done. The things you planned for us no one can recount to you; were I to speak and tell of them, they would be too many to declare.*
>
> – Psalm 40:5 NIV

I don't know about you, but these wonderful plans excite me, and I'm ready for them right NOW. But where to start?

The Bible says that the Lord makes known to us the mystery of His will according to His good pleasure, and He puts it into effect when the time is right.[4] It's not our job to take charge and make it happen; it's our duty to seek God for the plan, and then wait on His leading. Anyone with a brain knows how easy this is in word and how difficult it is in truth. Our human nature is to be impatient, and the conveniences of today's society only make it worse. The Lord warns us about impatient behavior:

> [Woe] *to those who say, "Let God hurry, let him hasten his work so we may see it."*
> – Isaiah 5:19 NIV

The Lord tells us that we are to seek His plans for us, set our minds on heavenly not earthly things, and look for His will not ours.[5] However, oftentimes we cannot comprehend God's plan, especially in its entirety. More often than not, God doesn't give us every piece of life's great puzzle, and so we find ourselves imagining what the final picture really looks like. While, this in itself is not dangerous, the problem comes when we begin to devise our own puzzle pieces to fill the voids. As you can guess, God has something to say about this too.

> *"Woe to the rebellious children," says the Lord, "who take counsel, but not of Me, And who devise plans, but not of My Spirit, That they may add sin to sin."*
> – Isaiah 30:1 NKJV

So let's recap what we <u>do</u> know:

* We know God has a plan for us – so, YES, you are called.

* We know to seek Him for the details and instructions.

* We know that we must wait on His leading.

My prayer for you is the same as the one in 2 Thessalonians 1:11:

I pray for you, that our God may count you worthy of His calling, and that by His power He may fulfill every good purpose of yours and every act prompted by your faith.

On page 45, there are questions that accompany this section. Take some time to carefully answer them.

Beyr Reyes, PhD

HOW PEOPLE RECEIVE THEIR CALLING

> *Therefore, brothers and sisters, make every effort to be sure of your calling and election. For by doing this you will never stumble into sin.*
> — 2 Peter 1:10 NET

Some people go to fortunetellers to learn the future, but I go to the Bible. When I want to know how God is going to speak to me, I just read how He's been doing it for thousands of years with other folks. If we know how God tends to call His children to His service, then we know what to look for in our own situation. Following are some examples to help you. (This is not an exhaustive list by any means.)

SAMUEL WAS CALLED BY THE VOICE OF GOD[6]

Samuel was raised in the temple from the time he was weaned from his mother's breast, and he grew up serving under Eli (the high priest). One night while alone in the Temple, Samuel heard someone calling for him. He immediately ran to Eli who was in his own bed and answered, "Here I am; you called me." Eli explained that he did not call the boy and told him to go back and lie down. Once more, Samuel heard someone calling him, so he ran back to Eli only to be told again to go back and lie down. The third time Samuel heard the calling and returned, Eli now realized what was going on. He told Samuel, "Go and lie down, and if He calls you, say, 'Speak, Lord, for your servant is listening.'" So Samuel did as he was told. The next time the Lord addressed Samuel, he was ready to listen and obey. This was the first time that God used Samuel as a prophet, and from that time on, the Lord was with him; He let none of Samuel's words fall to the ground in vain.

Moses Was Called From a Burning Bush[7]

Moses was tending his father-in-law's flock in the wilderness when he noticed a bush that was on fire but not being consumed by it. When the Lord saw that Moses was coming for a better look, He called to him from within the burning bush, and Moses said, "Here I am." As God explained to Moses that He was sending him to Egypt to deliver His people, Moses toned down his availability and began firing questions at God. His inquiries were like some of the ones we ask God:

* Who am I to do something like this?
* What if someone challenges my authority to do something like this?
* What if they don't believe me or listen to what I say?
* How am I supposed to do this when I don't have the skills to do it?

* Can't you send someone else besides me?

THE FIRST DISCIPLES WERE CALLED BY GOD IN PERSON

Peter, Andrew, James, and John were busy in their fishing jobs along the Sea of Galilee when Jesus approached them.[8] Jesus made a simple call to them: "Come, follow me and I will make you fishers of men." The four fishermen left their profession immediately and followed Him. In fact, James and John vacated in such a hurry that they left their father in the boat with the hired men. A little later, Jesus came across Matthew sitting in his tax collector's booth doing his daily job.[9] After Jesus made the simple call, "Follow me," Matthew got up and followed him just like the others did.

PAUL WAS CALLED AMIDST AFFLICTION[10]

Paul (also referred to as Saul) was hard at work persecuting the early Christians. While on his way to Damascus to get permission letters allowing him to take them prisoner at will, Paul saw a bright light from heaven suddenly flash around him. He fell to the ground and heard a voice say to him, "Why do you persecute me?" When Paul questioned the voice, it replied, "I am Jesus, whom you are persecuting. Go into the city, and you will be told what you must do." The men with Paul were speechless because they heard the voice but didn't see anyone. When Paul stood up, he realized that he was blind, and then the men led him by the hand into Damascus. Meanwhile, the Lord called to a disciple named Ananias in a vision. He told him to find Paul, place his hands on him, and pray for his sight to be restored. Ananias already knew of Paul and his reputation of persecuting Christians, so he questioned God. The Lord explained to him that He had chosen this man to proclaim His name to the Gentiles. Ananias did as he was instructed and as he prayed for Paul, something like scales fell from his eyes and he could see again. Paul got up and was baptized. After spending several days with the disciples in Damascus, he preached in the synagogues about Jesus and quickly began to experience persecution that he had once inflicted. Despite all the troubles he faced, just like the disciples, Paul left his livelihood, identity, and comfort zone. No hesitation. No questions.

OTHER METHODS

God uses several methods to call His children. We may hear Him calling directly from Heaven, through the still small voice of the Holy Spirit, or out of the mouths of other people. We may hear Him calling from the TV, a song, the Bible, or another book. He may summons us through dreams, visions, or words of prophesy. Regardless of our opinion about His methods, we must remain open to hearing from Him. For example, if He spoke to Solomon, Joseph (father of Jesus), and Daniel in dreams, then He can do the same with us. It is important that we don't find ourselves in a situation like Samuel where we don't recognize His voice.

What are common reactions to receiving a call from God? Well, not everyone responds like the disciples. Not everyone jumps on board without hesitation.

* Isaiah declared himself unworthy. [11]
* Jonah ran away. [12]
* Jeremiah said he was too young and inexperienced. [13]
* Ezekiel and Moses asked for concessions. [14]

Do you believe that you are called to write? Is it based on your heart's desire to write a book about your life? If so, I challenge you to rethink, re-pray, and then record what you hear from God. It is possible that God is really trying to prompt you to share your testimony with others. He may not be calling you to be a Christian author; instead, He may be calling you to evangelize and spread the Gospel.

For those of you who have no doubts concerning your calling to write for the Kingdom of God, I offer this advice:

> *When you pour something out of your heart, prepare to feel the emptiness in your soul.*
> – Beyr Reyes

On page 46, there are questions that accompany this section. Take some time to carefully answer them.

GOD WILL EQUIP YOU

May the God of peace ... equip you with everything good for doing His will, and may He work in us what is pleasing to him...

– Hebrews 13:20-22 NIV

The Word of God declares that we are His workmanship, created to do good works, which He has already prepared in advance for us to do.[15] His Word will equip us,[16] and the Lord will bless us abundantly, so that in all things at all times, having all that we need, we will succeed.[17]

We shouldn't waste our time or energy fretting about how to make everything happen the way we think it should go. When the crowd asked Jesus what they should do in order to do the works of God, Jesus answered, "Believe in the one He has sent."[18] We just need to trust God for what we need.

DESIRE

God gives us the desires of our heart.[19] This does not just mean that He gives us what we want, but that He also gives the want itself. He places desires deep within us and causes our plans to succeed. God equips us with desires for good works. So, if you have a desire to write about something, then by all means, go for it. (Well, of course, after you've prayed about it.)

Write what you enjoy. Solomon understood this when said that there is nothing better for a man than to enjoy his work because that is his reward.[20] It is a gift when God gives people wealth and possessions, and enables them to enjoy it, to accept their lot, and to be happy in their work.[21]

KNOWLEDGE AND WISDOM

God equips us with knowledge and wisdom that come from our experiences, our education, and His leading. Sometimes God will give us experiences so that we can write about them. For example, when the Israelites destroyed Amalek and his army, the Lord told Moses to write a memorial of the occasion.[22]

Education is another powerful tool. Lots of people spend many years in school learning skills, facts, and ways. The Lord expects us to use these gifts in our writing too. When we learn something, we need to be able to pass along the knowledge. God gave us a great example of this cycle when He taught Moses the law and then told him to go write it on tablets and teach others.[23]

Wisdom can be birthed by knowledge and learning, but the best kind comes from God. Human wisdom is limited. Even Solomon, the smartest man to ever live admitted that some things just cannot be reasoned by man. He said, "I have examined all this by wisdom and I'm determined to understand it, but it is beyond my grasp."[24] Some wisdom can ONLY come from God. Jesus said, "I will give you the words and wisdom that your enemy will not be able to resist or contradict."[25]

Sometimes God directs us to write about things we may not understand at the time. For example, John had to write about the things he saw in Heaven. The Lord said, "Therefore write what you saw, what is, and what will be."[26]

Talk about a daunting task! Nevertheless, John depended on the Holy Spirit to guide his hand, and so should we.

TESTIMONY

Your Testimony = Your History = His Story

Writers or not, we *all* are called to give a testimony of God's goodness, mercy, and saving grace. Jesus commanded us testify that He is the one whom God appointed as judge of the living and the dead.[27] Apostle Paul understood the importance of testifying when he said, "However, I consider my life worth nothing to me, if only I may finish the race and complete the task the Lord Jesus has given me—the task of testifying to the gospel of God's grace."[28] We should never be ashamed to testify about our Lord,[29] and need to share life-changing events that happen so that the work of God might be displayed through our life.[30]

Testimonies work. But why? People are most interested in true, human interest stories. They want to be able to identify with real people, who they can trust and relate to. A testimony builds a relationship, which makes your story more than just words; it touches their hearts. Also, people can argue with doctrine all day long, but they can't dispute the fact that your life is changed when it truly shows as you share your testimony. People crave that same peace and resolve in their own lives. In addition, because everyone suffers from the "gotta-tell-someone-else" syndrome, your testimony could lead to multiple lives being saved and changed as the story swims the social stream.

During ancient times when books were not available, God instructed the Israelites to erect memorial stones to commemorate certain events. For example, when the Israelites were crossing the Jordan, as the Lord held back the water, they picked up twelve stones (according to the number of tribes) from the middle of the river and carried them to Gilgal where they set up a stone memorial.[31] Years later, when the children asked about the stones, the people explained that the Lord God dried up the water of the Jordan to allow them to cross into the Promised Land.

In Galatians 1:11-17, Paul provides a testimony about his salvation and how he was called. Following are other types of testimonies.

- ** Life story
- ** Miracles
- ** Revelations
- ** Dreams and visions
- ** Deliverance
- ** Stewardship
- ** Blessings
- ** Healings
- ** Breakthroughs

Testimonies are an important tool especially for Christian writers. In fact, your testimony should be the very reason that you want to be a Christian writer. Whether directly or subtly, your personal testimonies will find a place in every book you write because you will deposit a piece of yourself in each one. Spend some time formulating stories about how God rescues, refreshes, and restores you daily. If you can't communicate your own story, then how can you communicate anything else?

Resources

God has already made available several resources for Christian writers including organizations, websites, and books. Following are several helpful ones.

Organizations

Christian Writers Guild (www.christianwritersguild.com) offers members one-on-one mentoring with writing professionals, free webinars, contests, the Writing for the Soul annual conference, critique services, a membership directory for connecting with other writers, articles about writing, writing opportunities, and much more. For information, call (866-495-5177) or email (contactus@christianwritersguild.com).

American Christian Fiction Writers (www.acfw.com) offers members writing courses, critique groups, contests, local chapters, the Christian Fiction Conference, fellowship and encouragement from other authors, prayer partners, and much more. For more information, contact them at webmaster@acfw.com, and your question will be forwarded to the appropriate person.

American Christian Writers offers members conferences and mentoring retreats across America, correspondence classes, local chapters, critique services, the Christian Communicator newsletter, the Advanced Christian Writers newsletter, and much more. They also offer a free writers' test. For information, call (800-21-WRITE) or email (ACWriters@aol.com).

Websites

Bible Gateway (www.biblegateway.com) provides online scripture in a wide variety of Bible versions.

The Blue Letter Bible (www.blueletterbible.org) is an online interactive reference library. One of its key offerings is the Hebrew-Greek Lexicon, which gives users immediate access to the original Hebrew and Greek words of each passage as well as cross-referencing of the original language to other passages throughout the entire Old and New Testament.

Christian Small Publishers Association (CSPA) (www.christianpublishers.net) provides information about small Christian publishers and the industry in general.

Association of Authors' Representatives (AAR) (www.aaronline.org) can be used to find a literary agent.

Readers' Favorite (www.readersfavorite.com) provides free reviews to authors. They also offer award contests and discounted services such as help with query letters, video trailers, publicity, digital conversion, and proofreading.

Books

Christian Writers Market Guide by Jerry B. Jenkins provides contact information for publishers of books and periodicals.

The Elements of Style, by Strunk, White, and Angell is a small but powerful book about correct grammar usage.

The Christian Writer's Manual of Style by Robert Hudson is a style guide for Christian writers.

Prophets Dictionary by Price Paula is a dictionary and reference book containing over 1,600 relevant definitions of terms and phrases.

The Complete Idiot's Guide to World Religions by Brandon Toropov and Father Luke Buckles provides information about world religions.

Handbook of Denominations in the United States by Craig Atwood provides information about church denominations.

HOLY SPIRIT

The Lord has given you a Helper, the Holy Spirit, who will abide with you forever,[32] so that you can say with confidence, "The Lord is my helper, and I will not be afraid."[33] He can provide you with everything covered and not covered in this book as well as many other things still unknown to man including connections, skills, people, and ideas.

On page 47, there are questions that accompany this section. Take some time to carefully answer them.

HOW TO KNOW WHAT TO WRITE

This is what the LORD, the God of Israel, says: "Write in a book all the words I have spoken to you."

– Jeremiah 30:2 NIV

First of all, you don't (and won't) always have a choice about what you write. Don't feel bad – the prophets didn't either.

Sometimes God will tell us what to write, even before we ask. For example he instructed Moses to write laws, blueprints, etc. He also commanded him to write a song and teach it to the Israelites.[34] After John visited Heaven, the Lord ordered him to write: "Write, therefore, what you have seen, what is now, and what will take place later."[35]

If you have no idea what to write or where to start, it could be that you are not called to do this, or perhaps that it's just not your season yet.

Before you embark on your calling to write, ask yourself these three questions:

    1. What are the goals and purpose of my writing?

2. To whom am I writing?
3. What type of writing should I do?

Purpose and Goals

Goals and purposes are inseparable and yet very distinct. You must keep both in mind when you write. The purpose is the reason you are writing, while the goal is how you intend to accomplish the purpose. For example, your purpose may be to use your experience and knowledge to help recovering addicts. Your goals would then be to teach them what the Word of God says about them and to encourage them. The most common goals in writing are to entertain, teach, evangelize, deliver, persuade, raise awareness, and encourage.

Take time to record your purpose of being a writer. This is sort of your mission statement. As you gain experience and age, your purpose may evolve. Let the Holy Spirit guide you in this and don't get locked into tradition and cadence.

Audience

Before you start writing, you need to decide whom the book is for. What group of people do you want to convey a message to? What people can you reach with commonality? Who will want to read your book? Who will read it even if they have to pay for it? The answer to these questions should all be the same. These people are your audience.

Once you identify your audience, you will need to study their characteristics, tendencies, and mindsets. Following are some general groups and things you need to consider when writing for them. Described below are five various audience groups.

1. New believers probably do not know church doctrine and church lingo (i.e., born again, slain in the spirit, praying through). Likewise, they probably don't understand church "protocol" like, for example, affluent people sit closer to the preacher and you can only add your offering to the plate with your left hand. (Ok – so I made up those examples, but you get the picture anyway.) Because new believers are spiritual children, they often lack discernment, so we must take extra care to explain things and not assume that they know complex theological things obvious to us. We will be held to a higher accountability when writing for this group, and need to be careful not to make them stumble in their faith.

2. Unsaved people (especially Americans) seem to be on guard around Christians and often defensive about the subject of Jesus (probably because they have been hurt by a Christian at some point in their life). Therefore, we must handle these people with lots of love and care. We cannot simply tell them to be a Christian; we have to show them with our actions, and in the case of writing, show them with our words. Many of them can quote popular proverbs but don't necessarily know that they come from the Bible (for example: like mother like daughter,[36] treat others like you want to be treated,[37] and spare the rod, spoil the child[38]). When you write for this group, you may consider paraphrasing verses so that they don't sound to "religious". Also, you need to consider how evangelic your tone will be. Will you use subtle Christian themes or be direct and get right to the point?

3. Christians are the obvious audience for Christian writers; however, this group can be the most difficult one for several reasons. Not everyone who calls himself or herself a Christian is actually a Christian. (Jesus makes this clear in Matthew 7:21-23.) Also, not every Christian is on the same spiritual level or aligned with your choice of doctrine or Bible version. When you write for certain groups of Christians, be familiar with their basic denominational beliefs and be careful around doctrinal issues unless they are the crux of the book.

4. Small groups require special considerations concerning the format of the writing. For example, the book or article may need any combination of the following items: discussion questions, pre-class reading assignments, room to take notes, and follow up activities. In addition, the topic for the writing must be something that easily leads to discussions.

5. Church pastors/teachers/leaders know the Word of God better than any other group. They need depth in the message and scripture to back it up. When writing for this group, consider incorporating the word origins in your key scriptures. Also, when you reference a scripture, choose the Bible version carefully. Not everyone is open to Bible versions other than the King James Version.

Everyone born has been classified as belonging to a particular generational group. Studies on these age groups reveal social and moral characteristics shared by the majority of their members. When you are writing, you need to be aware of which generational group comprises the preponderance of your audience and be cognizant of their nature. Described below are the four current groups.

1. Baby Boomers (born during the post–World War II baby boom, mid-1940s to mid-1960s) were the first generation to be analyzed and targeted by marketing, and they grew up alongside modern conveniences such as the telephone and television. They represent a large percentage in charitable giving. The Baby Boomer's perception is more holistic in nature, so they are interested in something as a whole, and not just the value of it or what it can do. They tend to make decisions based on emotional triggers.

2. Generation X (born between mid-1960s to early 1980s) is also known as the "latchkey kids" because they grew up in homes with both parents working. This generation is highly educated, active, balanced, happy, and family-oriented.[39] They openly acknowledge and embrace social diversity in terms of race, class, religion, ethnicity, culture, language, gender identity, and sexual orientation.[40] Unlike the Baby Boomers they are not interested in long-term careers, corporate loyalty, or status symbols; therefore, they tend to frequently change employment and even careers.

3. Millennials (born early 1980s to early 2000s) are also known as Generation Y and the Net Generation. They are technologically wise and comfortable with diverse groups. Confident and sociable, they have strong morals and a sense of civic duty. This generation is very flexible and does not show loyalty to brands. Sometimes they are referred to as Generation Me[41] because of their sense of entitlement and narcissism.

4. Generation Z (born ~2000 and after) is still defining their generation; however, early analysis shows that they are highly "connected" due to a lifelong use of communication and media technology. The outlook for this generation is not as bright as the previous ones. Some say this generation is the least likely one to believe in the American Dream (because they are growing up in a period of economic decline)[42] and are expected to be the first generation to earn less than their parents.[43] In addition, they experience blurred gender roles in their homes, and the future consequences of which are hard to predict.

A niche is a tightly focused audience. To illustrate what a niche is and how it is helpful, consider Jaime Marsman's hilarious book, *The Knitting Fairy: A Crabapple Yarns Mystery*. This book is a Christian-fiction mystery book, so right away you can get an idea of Jaime's general audience – Christians who like to read mysteries. Because the storyline involves a group of knitters in a yarn store, Jaime was able to find a niche. She solicited book reviews from leaders of the major knitting associations across the world and promoted her book on their message boards. Her book was immediately snapped up by knitters everywhere and they loved it (non-knitters love it too, including my husband, if you can believe that). The point is – although Jaime had a clear description of her general audience, she was able to hone in on readers in the knitting niche. Had she just targeted the Christian mystery lovers, she may have missed all these knitters. Furthermore, many of the knitters who bought the book were not Christians, and she may have missed these readers too.

If you can identify a niche for your writing, then you will be more successful at selling and distributing it. But more importantly, you may be able to reach people outside your general audience, thus resulting in a greater impact with your message. Consider niches for your writings and search for organizations relating to them.

Topics

Most writers write about what they know, whether it be something they learned from experience, school, or training. Experience is a great tool when picking a topic. God does not allow us to go through situations just for the fun of watching us flail about. He expects us to learn something that can later help us or others. Every aspect of our life, no matter how small, can be used to speak to others about their situation. Every place our eyes have swept over could be a potential scene in a fictional story, and every person we have met could be a character.

God quickens our hearts with certain interests and desires so that we will seek out the truths related to them. For this reason, many times you may find yourself writing about something that you simply like. Don't disregard a potential topic as trivial just because it seems like too much fun. Furthermore, God may put an interest in us about a something we know nothing about. Before we can write about a topic, we first must learn about it. There have been several times after having finished tons of research that I realized I may never write about that particular topic alone, but that the knowledge and scribbles may be used in another book still lurking in the air somewhere.

To get an idea of what topics are available in Christian writing, review the Book Industry Standards Advisory Committee (BISAC) codes, which are standard codes used by the publishing and retail industry to categorize a book based on its topic. (For example, the code FIC042040 is for books that are fiction Christian romances.)

A whopping 208 codes are just for books associated with religion. This doesn't include Bibles, which have ~175 separate codes. Also, this doesn't include other religion books nested in other genres (for example, there are nine codes for various types of fiction that's Christian derived.) See the BISAC codes on the Book Industry Study Group website (www.bisg.org/what-we-do-0-136-bisac-subject-headings-list-major-subjects.php) to see various topics in Christian writing. Make a list of the ones that best fit your calling.

TYPES OF WRITING

What you write greatly depends on whom you are writing for because the type of writing conveys the purpose for the writing. The Bible offers many great illustrations of different types of writings and how they are used.

- ** Fiction (even Jesus told parables)
- ** History and biographies (i.e., annuals of the kings, Chronicles, Genesis, the four gospels)
- ** How to guides and standard operating procedures (God gave Moses instructions of how to build the tabernacle)
- ** Rules and guidelines (i.e., Leviticus, the Ten Commandments)
- ** Letters to people (i.e., letters by Peter and Paul)

- ** Teaching and instructional writing (i.e., Paul's writings)
- ** Songs and poems (i.e., Psalms)
- ** Genealogy
- ** Decrees
- ** Eye-witness accounts
- ** Prophesy, dreams, and visions

When trying to decide what type of writing to do, ask yourself these questions. What do I like to read? (This is a good place to start. You will be familiar with what is expected for that genre.) Which type of writing will be the easiest and clearest way to convey my message? What type of writing does my specific audience prefer?

On page 48, there are questions that accompany this section. Take some time to carefully answer them.

WHAT IT MEANS TO BE A WRITER FOR GOD

*Being a writer for God
will cost you more than you could ever reckon
and give you more than it would ever cost.*
— Beyr Reyes

THE COST OF WRITING FOR GOD

Writing for God will cost you time, energy, comfortableness, resources, and so much more.

Higher Accountability

Christian writers are representatives of Jesus and the Word of God. We must do our best to present ourselves to God as one approved, a workman who does not need to be ashamed, and one who correctly handles the word of truth.[44] We must live a life worthy of the calling we have received.[45]

Everyone will be judged in the end; however, teachers and leaders in the Kingdom will be judged more strictly.[46] The more authority and responsibility we are given in this life, the additional accountability we inherit. If all we write about are the blessings of God and don't balance it with the warnings of eternal death without salvation through Jesus, then everyone who dies in sin on our watch, their blood will be on our hands and we will be accountable for it.[47] Writing is a powerful gift in the Kingdom because one publication, or even a single post on social media, can reach millions of people at a time. Today's words are forever traceable and can travel the world as fast as a click. God entrusts His workers with much and then demands an accounting of their deeds.[48] There is power in you words so be careful what you write. The Bible warns us: "Woe to those who decree unrighteous decrees, who write misfortune, which they have prescribed."[49]

Accelerated Maturity

As official representatives of God's Kingdom, Christian writers are expected to operate at a higher level of maturity – expected to walk the walk, and not just talk the talk. We must live what we say we believe. James 1:22 says to be sure we are doers of the word and not just hearers, lest we be deceived. What does this really mean? It means it's time to grow up and go deeper.

In order to be credible writers, we need to practice what we preach. We must rid ourselves of all malice, guile, hypocrisy, envy, and slander.[50] Maturity comes by training ourselves in discernment, and the only way to do this is to know what the Bible says.[51] It's ludicrous to think how many people who have claimed to be Christians for years and yet have never read the book they follow and defend. Do they even know what they signed up for? As a Christian writer, you better not fall into this category, or you will be found out in a hurry.

Another part of maturity is being willing to submit to authority. Before I release each new book, I have people in my church leadership read it and provide their approval. If there is something in the book that does not line up with scripture, I expect them to tell me. I take it very seriously that I am accountable for every word I write. I don't want to stand before God one day and try to explain why I led people astray. I'm pretty sure that "I didn't know that was wrong" will NOT work as an excuse. It will be much easier to accept the criticism from my leaders or other trusted confidents than it will be to hear it from my Heavenly Father.

Spiritual Warfare

The minute you put yourself out there as a Christian writer, you will pop up on the enemy's radar. Unfortunate, I know. Instead of denying it, get ready for it, because the enemy comes to steal, kill, and destroy.[52] The Bible clearly states that our struggle is not against flesh and blood, but it is one against the spiritual forces of evil.[53] We are commanded to guard the good deposit that is entrusted to us, and do it with the help of the Holy Spirit.[54] We start this by putting on the armor of God[55] and praying at all times in the Spirit.[56]

Anytime we sow the Word of God into someone's life, the enemy comes immediately to steal it.[57] The same is true in our own life. The very instant we take a stand, claim allegiance, or declare a word, we will be tested on that very thing. And if that's not enough, when the anointing of God falls upon you and God makes it apparent that He is pleased, you may be driven into a wilderness experience where you will battle alone. It happened to Jesus, you know.[58]

The hardest battle Christian writers will face is the one inside their own mind. We are taught to be humble creatures, and yet being a writer requires a knack for self-promotion. Well, how do you do decrease self and while increasing the sales of your books and other writings? I have spent untold hours mentoring and teaching other writers how to promote themselves and handle the media. I quickly noticed that Christians struggle more with this task of being an author than any other. The battle of false humility, self-promotion, and pride can confound even the most faithful at heart.

Time and Money

It's a gift when God gives people wealth and possessions, and then enables them to enjoy it, to accept their lot, and to be happy in their work.[59] We must always remember that everything belongs to the Lord.[60] The Bible directs us to give a tithe of everything we receive back to our Lord.[61] (He's the one who gave it to us in the first place.) We are also instructed to honor God with our wealth and the firstfruits of all our increase[62] and to give alms (charity) offerings to others.[63] Do you follow these financial commands? God asks, "Will a man rob God? Yet you rob me. But you ask, 'How do we rob you?' In tithes and offerings … Bring the whole tithe into the storehouse…" (Malachi 3:8-10, NIV)

Money is not the only thing we are supposed to give. God doesn't just want our currency; He wants our life and time with us. Many Christians try to set aside time every day to fellowship with God, to read His Word, and to pray. For Christian writers, the lines between work and time with God may get fuzzy. In other words, writing for God is not the same as spending time with Him. For example, doing research on your topic in the Bible is not the same thing as hanging out with God in His Word. Writers must be careful to not allow writing to become an idol in their lives. It must NEVER come before God. Sounds easy, but I promise that it's not.

The Truth Sometimes Hurts

You may not have seen the movie *A Few Good Men*, but you probably recognize a memorable quote from it: "You Can't Handle the Truth!" The fact is – not everyone wants to hear the truth. Some people just want their ears tickled.

The Bible says that a time will come when people will not endure sound doctrine; but instead will seek after their own lusts and only entertain the teaching from those who tell them what they want to hear.[64] For example, the Bible states that murder is wrong, but many people (including Christians) make an exception for unborn children. Another example is homosexuality, which is something that the Bible clearly indicates is a sin.

Not everyone who reads your writing will receive the entire message you offer. Some just want a quick fix and end up foregoing the fullness of the matter. Luke 17: 11-19 tells a story about ten lepers Jesus encountered. They cried out to Him for mercy, and He sent them to the priest. As they went, they were cleansed. However, one of the men saw that he was healed, turned back, and with a loud voice glorified Jesus. He fell down on his face at Jesus' feet, giving him thanks. And Jesus said to him, "Your faith has made you whole." This man not only received healing from his disease like the other nine men, but unlike them, Jesus made him whole by repairing all the damage the disease had done. The other nine men were content with a quick fix.

Sometimes we are called to deliver bad news. For example, the book of Daniel tells us that King Belshazzar was hosting a great feast in the royal palace when suddenly, God made a human hand appear and write a message to the king on the plaster wall. The message was *mene, mene, tekel, parsin*, which Daniel later interpreted to mean God had numbered the days of the king's reign and ended it. He had been weighed on the scales and found to be lacking. His kingdom would be divided and given to others.[65] Now I don't know about you, but that is not the kind of message that I would want to deliver.

We must understand that if people won't receive a message from the Lord, then they certainly won't accept it from us. No matter how stern the warning or how painful the punishment, some people just won't budge. Jeremiah faced this over and over again, and when the people would not listen to him, he even tried the leaders, all to no avail.

> *Lord, do not your eyes look for truth? You struck them, but they felt no pain; you crushed them, but they refused correction. They made their faces harder than stone and refused to repent I thought, "These are only the poor; they are foolish, for they do not know the way of the LORD, the requirements of their God. So I will go to the leaders and speak to them; surely they know the way of the LORD, the requirements of their God." But with one accord they too had broken off the yoke and torn off the bonds.*
>
> *– Jeremiah 5:3-5 NIV*

The truth often offends, so don't get your feelings hurt when people don't accept it. Remember that they are rejecting the Word of God, not you, so do not take it personal. However, DO take it personal when it is your heart that God is speaking to. There have been times when I had to write something that I myself was still overcoming. The book, *Make a Choice*, was written by me to me. While others may get revelation upon reading it, I assure you that the pain was all mine when writing it. Sometimes being a writer for God means that you write for an audience of two: God and yourself.

ADVANTAGES OF WRITING FOR GOD

Writing for God is extremely rewarding. However, I purposely made this section shorter than the previous one describing the costs. This is because I am trying to make sure to not "sell" you on becoming a Christian writer. I want you to choose this path not for all the blessings, but because you know without a doubt it's what God wants for you.

Anyone who has discovered their calling in this life will tell you that it's the most fulfilling thing ever. Personally, I get immense satisfaction when someone shares how something I wrote renewed their mind or transformed their life. But, this type of fulfillment is only a fraction of what I will get when I hear my Lord say, "Well done my good and faithful servant."[66]

The Bible offers us about 8,000 blessings or promises and tells us that God blesses us in all the works of our hands.[67] This one sentence alone outweighs the entire previous section about the costs of being a Christian writer. The Bible says that we will be rewarded for our good works both on this earth and in Heaven. On earth we will experience His favor[68] and receive gifts of wealth, possessions, and enjoyment in our toil.[69] Sometimes we are rewarded by seeing immediate change in people's life after they read our writings. Other times our writings are only the seeds that someone else will water and see grow. Regardless of the wonderful rewards in this life, they will never compare to the ones in eternity. The Bible tell us that the Son of Man will come with His angels in the glory of His Father, and then He will reward each person according to what he has done.[70] One day, we will receive a crown of glory that will never fade.[71]

On page 49, there are questions that accompany this section. Take some time to carefully answer them.

Beyr Reyes, PhD

CHOOSE YOUR PATH WISELY

Stand at the crossroads and look; ask for the ancient paths, ask where the good way is, and walk in it, and you will find rest for your souls...
— Jeremiah 6:16 NIV

The life of a writer is exhausting, vulnerable, and always receiving of criticism. It is not surprising then, that when faced with the choice Jeremiah 6:16 presents, many people chose the last few words of the verse instead: *...But you said, "We will not walk in it."*

The Bible says that man's ways are in full view of the Lord, and He examines all man's paths.[72] Everyone has choices in this life, and God knows what each one entails and produces. We can embrace the path God has for us or we can reject it. No one can make this decision for us. God knows the good way and He has already given us everything we need to be successful.[73] However, it is up to us to make every effort to confirm our calling.[74] It doesn't stop there, either. We must be sure to not stray from our path. If you ever wonder whether you are on God's ordained path or not, then drop to your knees and bow humbly in prayer – your nose will hit it every time.

Beyr Reyes, PhD

Beware of Obstacles on Your Path

What draws the attention of the enemy faster than a key stroke? Someone writing about the goodness of God. So, prepare yourself. The enemy will show up to either bring you to a halt or divert your course. As a Christian writer, you will face many obstacles dealing with time, health, money, and life in general. Most of these take considerable orchestration by the enemy to have an effect on us. However, there is one impediment in his arsenal that is fast, easy to use, and rather debilitating – it's called writer's block, and it trips up writers all the time and stops them right in their tracks. The enemy also uses diversion to distract you from your path. It is important to consider these two snags and have your defenses in tact when the enemy comes prowling around.

Writer's Block

Writer's block is a condition in which a writer loses the ability to produce a new work or to continue writing an existing one. Writer's block is NOT the same thing as writer's fatigue. Time and rest will cure fatigue, but a block has underlying issues. Some common causes of writer's block include:

- ** Wanting to do something else other than writing
- ** Not wanting to write about the topic (i.e., too painful)
- ** Not liking the topic
- ** Not knowing enough about topic
- ** Fear of saying something wrong
- ** Getting resentful
- ** Being blocked by God
- ** Lacking gumption

- ** Taking on the spirit of the writing (i.e., getting depressed when writing about the topic of depression)

Writer's block can last for a day, a week, or even a season in life. If you find yourself unable to write for long periods of time, don't worry or shame yourself. Many times, these long respites can be excellent opportunities for reading and fellowshipping with God instead of writing. Hebrews 4:10 reminds us that when we enter God's rest, we also rest from our own work, just as God did from His. Also, take note that not all writer's block comes from the enemy. Sometimes God will shut us down for a period of time. For example, He closed Hanna's womb[75] and shut Zechariah's mouth[76] until the time was right.

To overcome enemy-caused writer's block, try some of these approaches.

- ** Take a break for a predetermined amount of time (i.e., tell yourself that for the next two weeks you won't even think about the book at all and follow through with the plan)
- ** Write on another topic
- ** Read a book unrelated to the topic or genre of your writing
- ** Try something new, like a hobby or sport
- ** Pray
- ** Research more about the topic, especially from a different angle. (For example, if writing about a heavy topic like depression, find some funny stories, poems, or cartoons about it.)

Sometimes we just need to kick-start our creative gumption. An easy way to do this is to make your writing project look different. For example, change the paper or background color of your screen. Make the font a fun color other than black. Change the page size so the document flow becomes unfamiliar to you. You can also change your approach to the writing. For example, change time of day or place you usually write; alternate the way you write (i.e., computer vs. handwriting); try a different writing style (i.e., outlining vs. free flow); use concept mapping.

The whole purpose of writer's block is to prevent you from moving forward. No matter which remedy you use for the problem, just don't give up. Even if you have to slow down, do like Dori says, "Just keep swimming; just keep swimming."

Wandering Path

Imagine a hiker on a nature trail. What are some things that may prompt him to leave the path? Perhaps seeing something shiny or something novel and interesting alongside it, maybe second guessing the path and wondering whether he is on the right one, and of course, backtracking. All these reasons affect the paths of our lives too.

What are some shiny things that would distract Christian writers from their path? Well, the obvious is money. Allow me to blow your mind with some numbers. An average book will sell about 1000 to 3000 copies over its lifetime. If the retail price is $10 and the royalty rate for the writer is 10% of net sales, then he or she stands to make approximately $0.20 per book for a $200 to $600 total. Not enough to make someone rich. The point is – unless you are the next best-selling author, writing won't line your pockets with gold. When authors reach this realization, they question whether it is worth it and are tempted to give up the writing path for one that pays more money.

Writers can be led astray with novel and interesting things too. Beware of newly found "spiritual" principles and ideas. Be sure to test them against scripture before you use them. Let the Word of God be a light for your path.[77] And for the sake of all goodness, do not assume that you are not susceptible to religious deception. If Eve, who walked personally with God in the garden on a daily basis, could be deceived, then so could you. The Apostle Paul said, "But I am afraid that just as Eve was deceived by the serpent's cunning, your minds may somehow be led astray from your sincere and pure devotion to Christ."[78] Be on the lookout for false teachers and prophets because the enemy masquerades as an angel of light, and his servants as ministers of righteousness.[79]

Wondering in your mind leads to wandering along your path. Did you catch that? Thoughts of fear, insecurity, and self-doubt will cause someone to swerve to the right or left. Caustic contemplations like these will spur you to rethink decisions and crisscross your own path.

Spending time in the past will cause you to backtrack on your path. The enemy likes it when we live in the past because we become ineffective in the present. Science has shown that thinking about the past and planning for the future use the same area of the brain. Therefore, if you are always thinking about the past, it is physiologically difficult, if not impossible, to plan for the future. Consider the Israelites who were always remembering Egypt fondly and threatening to go back. They ended us wandering in the desert for forty years which resulted in a whole generation missing the Promised Land.

The Bible illustrates grave consequences for wandering. Proverbs 15:10 says that stern discipline awaits him who leaves the path, and he who hates correction will die.[80] If you wander along your path, then you may find yourself in the same situation as Balaam – between a rock and a hard place with a sword blocking the way.[81]

SWEEP YOUR PATH WITH PRAYER

The best way to keep a path clear is to sweep it clean of obstacles. Pray over your writing before you start a project, each time before you sit down to write, during the editing process, and every time the Lord brings it to your mind.

Beyr Reyes, PhD

When you receive the final copy before it's released to the public, pray for God to open every mind and heart to the message you are sending forth. In between writing projects, pray that God would plant new ideas into your spirit. Pray for the success of your writings and that your path will be straight.

Here is my prayer for your path:

> *Show them your ways, O Lord,*
> *Teach them your paths that are right.*[82]
> *Direct them in the path of your commands,*
> *For there they will find delight.*[83]
>
> *Make level paths for their feet*
> *And take only ways that are firm.*[84]
> *Lord, broaden the path beneath them,*
> *So that their ankles do not turn.*[85]
>
> *When their spirit grows faint within them,*
> *It is You who knows their way.*[86]
> *Restore their soul and guide them*
> *In paths of righteousness for Your name.*[87]
>
> *May they keep their feet from every evil path*
> *So that they might obey Your Word.*[88]
> *Lord, thank you for listening*
> *And that this prayer has been heard.*[89]

On page 51, there are questions that accompany this section. Take some time to carefully answer them.

QUESTIONS AND REFLECTIONS

Beyr Reyes, PhD

Questions from "Are You Called?"

1. Do you really believe that you are called for great works? Even if you don't know for what yet?

2. Do you feel worthy to be called? Do you feel worthy to be a worker and representative for God? If not, why not?

3. Consider the following verse: [Woe] *to those who say, "Let God hurry, let him hasten his work so we may see it."* (Isaiah 5:19 NIV). Have you ever been guilty of trying to hurry God? What was the result?

Beyr Reyes, PhD

Questions from
"How People Receive Their Calling"

1. Have you been called to do something? (If not, go to question 4.) What was it?

2. How did you receive the calling?

3. What was your initial response?

4. If you have no idea what your role is in God's Kingdom, what can you do to find out?

5. Do you think it is possible that you failed to hear your calling? If so, was it intentional or accidental?

6. If you missed your calling the first time and now recognize this, what can (and will) you do?

Questions from "God Will Equip You"

God equips us with desires, skills, education, life experiences, and other resources. Sometimes we are put in charge of things, because we are skillful at them.[90]

1. What desires has God placed in your heart? What do you love to do? On a scale of 1 to 10, how much do you enjoy writing?

2. What activities give you the greatest pleasure? For example, art, sports, sewing.

3. List your top ten skills. Which of these would help you to be a Christian writer?

4. What things have you been educated in (either by a class or self-taught)? Which of these would help you to be a Christian writer?

5. List major life events have you experienced and how each of these would help you with writing.

6. See the list of the different kinds of testimonies. Write a personal testimony for each of these types.

7. Looking back at your responses in this section, does it appear that God has equipped you to be Christian writer? If so, explain your answer. If not, what do you lack and how would you get it?

Beyr Reyes, PhD

Questions from "How to Know What to Write"

1. What is your purpose of being a writer?

2. What kind of people can you reach with commonality? In other words, what kind of audience would relate to you?

3. Who will want to read your writings? Who will read them even if it costs money?

4. Who will be your audience?

5. List special considerations for other general audiences such as parents, kids, veterans, etc.

6. Visit the BISG website (www.bisg.org/what-we-do-0-136-bisac-subject-headings-list-major-subjects.php) and make a list of BISAC codes for topics that would best fit your call to write.

7. What types of writing interest you? How are the topics in question 6 similar or different to the types of writings you like to read yourself?

Questions from "What it Means to be a Writer for God"

1. The Bible has a strong warning about adding or omitting any words from its meaning.[91] How does this warning make you feel about being a Christian writer?

2. James 1: 23 (NIV) states: *"For if someone merely listens to the message and does not live it out, he is like someone who gazes at his own face in a mirror. For he gazes at himself and then goes out and immediately forgets what sort of person he was. But the one who peers into the perfect law of liberty and fixes his attention there, and does not become a forgetful listener but one who lives it out—he will be blessed in what he does."* Does the person you see in the mirror look like the one who writes your books? In other words, do you live up to what you write about?

3. Mature Christians are not easily offended.[92] How good are you at taking criticism of your writings? Do you get defensive? Offended?

4. The Bible tells us several times to humble ourselves and to not be full of pride. (Read 1 Peter 5:6, 2 Corinthians 3:5, Proverbs 27:2, Matthew 23:12, Romans 12:3, Colossians 2:18, and Philippians 2:3-11.) How will you handle praise for your writings?

5. What is the difference between true and false humility? How do you recognize each one? How can we be truly humble?

6. How will you differentiate time in the Word doing research for your topic from time in the Word fellowshipping with your Heavenly Father? What are signs that your writing is becoming an idol and coming before the Lord?

7. What kinds of earthly and heavenly rewards from God and people are you expecting to receive for your writings? In the spirit of Acts 20:35, how much of your writings will you do just for the love of others and receive no recognition or financial compensation?

8. Will you write using your real name or a pen name? Explain your choice.

9. How will you react when it seems like your writings are not having an effect for the Kingdom? How does 1 Corinthians 3:8 possibly explain the situation?

10. How will you share the truth with those who do not want to hear it? Don't just say "...with love". Provide a detailed approach.

Questions from "Choose Your Path Wisely"

1. When looking at your path stretched out straight before you, you see that as it traverses into the distance ahead, it ends in a single point. What is the point of your path? Where is it taking you and what is its purpose?

2. What obstacles will you face in your calling to write? Name some not mentioned in this book.

3. If money isn't a big reward for writing for God, then what is?

4. Do you spend your time wondering what could have been and reliving past mistakes? How does this affect your path today?

5. Have you ever wandered away from your path? What were the consequences?

Final Questions

1. Are you truly called to be a writer for the Kingdom? How do you know for sure?

2. What does this mean for your current career? Your family? Your church?

3. How are you equipped to be a Christian writer?

4. What is your next step on this writing path?

ABOUT THE AUTHOR

BEYR REYES received her doctorate degree in Biomedical Science and has nearly 200 publications in science and medicine. She has spent the last several years teaching and mentoring Christian writers, and even started ShadeTree Publishing to provide a more accessible publishing venue for them and to serve as a birthing station for their careers.

See Beyr's author page at
http://www.shadetreepublishing.com/beyr-reyes.html.

Other Books by Beyr Reyes, PhD

Fast Answers: When You Need Answers Now

You may be asking whether the world needs another book about fasting, and the answer is YES, because THIS book is different. Other books tell you why to fast or explain the importance thereof, but leave you guessing how to even start. This book puts legs on your intentions so that you can walk it out. "Fast Answers" has mapped fasting plans with a clear starting point, destination, and goal. The plans come in one-, three-, or seven-day varieties and are tailored to specific prayer needs. No longer will you fumble your way through a fast. With this book, you will find your way to the answers you need right now. This book isn't about fast answers (as in quick ones). It's about fast answers (as in seeking God ones).

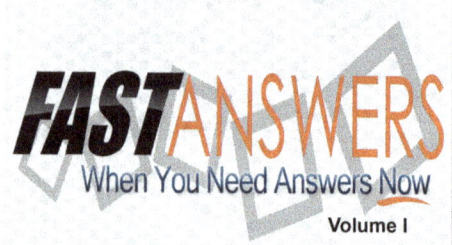

Download cooresponding app at
www.iNeedFastAnswers.com

Subject Your Flesh

Need to get control of your life? Tired of constant dieting? Fed up with bad habits? Subjection is the answer that lasts. Learn how to eradicate the problem areas in your life. Take control of your flesh and turn your life around using the Word of God.

Beyr Reyes, PhD

Make A Choice

This book is a continuum of revelation designed to challenge your foundational beliefs and then challenge you to stand on those beliefs. In Unit 1 (Choose Your Beliefs), you will ask yourself questions like: Is God really God? Is Jesus God? Is the Bible true? In Unit 2 (Live Like You Mean It), you will ask yourself: Am I really a Christian? Am I really saved? Am I really forgiven? All along the way, you will make decisions that will affect your life forever.

The Big Picture

Most folks know the stories about Creation, the Jewish nation, and Jesus, but they don't know how all these things are connected. This book is a broad perspective of the Bible that will help the beginner place events and their purposes. For the readers who always have their heads buried in certain passages, this book is a refreshing step back to help illuminate the big picture.

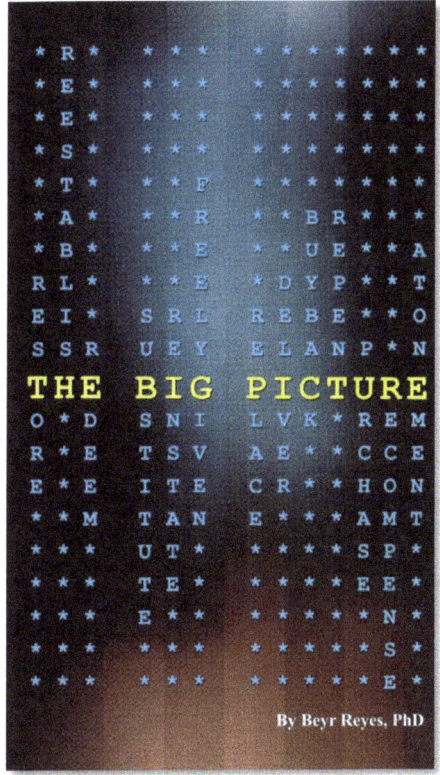

Beyr Reyes, PhD

REFERENCES

1 Acts 10:41-43
2 Jeremiah 1:5
3 Jeremiah 29:11
4 Ephesians 1:9-10
5 Colossians 3:2
6 1 Samuel 3
7 Exodus 3 and 4
8 Mark 1:16-20
9 Matthew 9:9-11
10 Acts 9
11 Isaiah 6
12 Jonah 1:3
13 Jeremiah 1
14 Ezekiel 4:14 and Exodus 3
15 Ephesians 2:10
16 2 Timothy 3:17
17 2 Corinthians 9:8 NIV
18 John 6:28-29
19 Psalm 20:4
20 Ecclesiastes 3:22
21 Ecclesiastes 5:19
22 Exodus 17:14
23 Exodus 24:12
24 Ecclesiastes 7:23
25 Luke 21:15
26 Revelation 1:19
27 Acts 10:42
28 Acts 20:24 NIV
29 2 Timothy 1:8
30 John 9:3
31 Joshua 4
32 John 14:16
33 Hebrews 13:6
34 Deuteronomy 31:19
35 Revelation 1:19 NIV
36 Ezekiel 16:44
37 Luke 6:30-32
38 Proverbs 13:24
39 Dawson, Alene (2011-10-26). "Study says Generation X is balanced and happy". CNN. Retrieved 2012-06-25.
40 Isaksen, Judy L. (2002). "Generation X". St. James Encyclopedia of Pop Culture.
41 Twenge, Ph.D., Jean (2006). Generation Me. New York, NY: Free Press (Simon & Schuster). ISBN 978-0-7432-7697-9.
42 DeBord, Mathew. "A new generation gets a name: Plurals." DeBord Report. April 30, 2012. Horovitz, Bruce. "Generation Whatchamacallit." USA Today.
43 Shapiro, Evan. "TV: An Intervention." Huffington Post, June 5, 2012
44 2 Timothy 2:15 NIV
45 Ephesians 4:1
46 James 3: 3
47 Ezekiel 3:20
48 Luke 12:48
49 Isaiah 10:1 NKJV
50 1 Peter 2:1
51 Hebrews 5: 14
52 John 10:10
53 Ephesians 6: 12
54 2 Timothy 1:14
55 Ephesians 6: 11
56 Ephesians 6: 18
57 Mark 4:15
58 Mark 1:10-13
59 Ecclesiastes 5:19
60 Psalms 24:1
61 Leviticus 27:30
62 Proverbs 3:9
63 Luke 12:33
64 2 Timothy 4:3
65 Daniel 5:5, 24-28
66 Matthew 25:21
67 Deuteronomy 2:7
68 Psalm 11:7
69 Ecclesiastes 5:19
70 Matthew 16:27 NET
71 1 Peter 5: 4
72 Proverbs 5:21 NIV
73 2 Peter 1:3
74 2 Peter 1:10
75 1 Samuel 1:5
76 Luke 1: 20
77 Psalm 119:105
78 2 Corinthians 11:3 NIV
79 2 Corinthians 11:14-15
80 Proverbs 15:10 NIV
81 Numbers 22:24-26
82 Psalm 25:4
83 Psalm 119:35 NIV
84 Proverbs 4:26
85 Psalm 18:36
86 Psalm 142:3
87 Psalm 23:3
88 Psalm 119:101
89 Psalm 66:19
90 1 Chronicles 15:22
91 Revelation 22:18-19
92 Psalm 119:165

www.ingramcontent.com/pod-product-compliance
Lightning Source LLC
Chambersburg PA
CBHW071222070526
44584CB00019B/3123